U.S. ARMED FORCES

The U.S. ARMY

MICHAEL BENSON

LERNER PUBLICATIONS COMPANY / MINNEAPOLIS

CHAPTER OPENER PHOTO CAPTIONS

Cover: A U.S. Army tank crew patrols the Kuwaiti desert near the end of the 1991 Persian Gulf War.

Ch. 1: U.S. Army pilots in a Blackhawk helicopter scout a factory area near Baghdad for military targets during the 2003 war in Iraq.

Ch. 2: Two recruiting sergeants stand by a minivan displaying the army's slogan: A Force of One.

Ch. 3: A drill sergeant pushes recruits through physical training. Drills teach soldiers physical and mental discipline, as well as to work as a team.

Ch. 4: These soldiers are securing a bucket loader onto a truck. The loader will later be air-dropped into a location where it's needed.

To Muriel Dech, who gave me a shove

Acknowledgments
Thanks to Tim Treu, David Jacobs, Jake Elwell, Peg Goldstein, Timothy W. Larson, Staff Sergeant Eric S. Butler, and Jerry G. Burgess, Director, U.S. Army Women's Museum

Lerner Publications Company
A division of Lerner Publishing Group
241 First Avenue North
Minneapolis, MN 55401

Website address: www.lernerbooks.com

Library of Congress Cataloging-in-Publication Data

Benson, Michael.
      The U.S. Army / by Michael Benson
         p.   cm. — (U.S. Armed Forces)
   Includes biographical references and index.
      Contents: History — Recruitment — Training — Life in the Army.
      ISBN: 0–8225–1645–4 (lib. bdg. : alk. paper)
      1. United States. Army—Juvenile literature. 2. United States. [1. United States Army.]
   I. Title. II. Series: U.S. Armed Forces (Series : Lerner Publications)
   UA25.B39 2005
   355'.00973—dc22   2003023459

Manufactured in the United States of America
2 3 4 5 6 7 — JR — 10 09 08 07 06 05

CONTENTS

chapter ONE
HISTORY

IN THE SPRING OF 2003, the United States wanted to remove dictator Saddam Hussein from power in Iraq. The U.S. Army, along with other military units, was sent to get the job done in this Middle Eastern nation. Army units arrived by plane and ship at military bases around the Middle East. They came from the United States and other nations.

Starting on March 19, 20,000 U.S. Army soldiers marched across the Iraqi desert, heading toward Baghdad, Iraq's capital. Some of the soldiers fired shells, bombs, and bullets at the enemy. But other soldiers didn't do any fighting. Instead, they worked as message senders, doctors, and priests. Some of the soldiers were men, and some were women. The army was like a moving, fighting city. It had its own churches, medical units, post office, and kitchens. It carried equipment and supplies.

The United States has the most powerful army in the world. It easily defeated Saddam Hussein's army during the 2003 war in Iraq. After the main fighting was over, many army soldiers remained in Iraq to do peace-keeping work and to help rebuild the nation.

Two U.S. Army soldiers prepare to enter and search a building in Pir Ahmad, Iraq, during the 2003 war.

AROUND THE GLOBE DEFENDING FREEDOM

The U.S. Army has been fighting military battles for more than 200 years—right from the first days of our nation's history. As U.S. involvement in world affairs has grown, the U.S. Army has grown too. It protects U.S. property, ideals, and citizens all over the world, even in faraway places such as Iraq.

The army is the branch of the U.S. military that handles land operations. The army works with other branches of the military—the U.S. Navy, Air Force, Marine Corps, and Coast Guard—during military campaigns. The army is the largest branch of the military, with about 600,000 soldiers on active duty. It is also the strongest military force in the world. The U.S. Army has a long history—as old as the United States itself.

A paratrooper (a soldier trained to skydive) from the army's 508th Airborne Battalion prepares to jump from an airplane.

A group of American colonists (settlers) walks to church under the protection of armed guards in New England during the 1600s. Colonists formed some of the earliest military groups in North America.

ROOTS OF THE U.S. ARMY

In the 1600s, groups of settlers arrived in North America from Great Britain. The settlers were seeking land and religious freedom. The first settlements were governed by rulers back in Great Britain.

The North American settlers soon found themselves at war. First, they fought with Native Americans whose ancestors had lived in North America for thousands of years. The Native Americans did not want British settlers taking over their ancient homelands. To fight and defend themselves against Native Americans, the settlers formed militias, or citizen military forces.

In the late 1700s, the settlers went to war to win independence from Great Britain. They created the Continental Army, later called the U.S. Army, on June 14, 1775. Its job was to fight the British in North America. General George Washington was the army's commander in chief.

The war came to be called the American Revolution, or Revolutionary War (1775–1783). Most soldiers fought on foot. Using rifles called muskets, they lined up in long rows to fire at British soldiers. Then they closed in for hand-to-hand combat using bayonets (steel blades attached to their muskets). Some soldiers, called cavalrymen, attacked the enemy on horseback.

By 1783 the Continental Army had defeated the British forces. The United States of America was a new, independent nation. George Washington became

WOMEN IN THE ARMY

During the American Revolution, some women worked as nurses. A few even joined the soldiers on the battlefield, although women were not officially allowed to fight. Molly Pitcher *(above)* is the made-up name of a woman who fought in 1778 at the Battle of Monmouth during the Revolution. During the Civil War (1861–1865), some women joined the army disguised as men. In World War I (1914–1918), women served in the army as nurses and office workers. During World War II (1939–1945), the army created a separate unit called the Women's Army Corps (WAC). WACs worked as secretaries, cooks, engineers, nurses, and doctors. But they were still not allowed in combat. In the 2000s, women serve in almost every army position, including jobs that take them close to the battlefield.

the first president of the United States. As president, he
remained the army's commander in chief.

THE EARLY YEARS

At first, the U.S. Army was made up of many local
militias. Each militia had its own uniforms and
weapons. Some weapons were of poor quality. To
create a stronger army, the U.S. government created
the Department of War in 1789. This department
made sure that the army was well organized.

After the Revolution, the army helped explore the
American wilderness. From 1804 to 1806, army
officers Meriwether Lewis and William Clark led an
expedition to explore North America west of the
Mississippi River.

A local militia, part of the early U.S. Army, stands ready
to defend its town in the late 1700s.

Soon after, the army fought—and won—a second war with the British: the War of 1812 (1812–1815). The war started over disagreements about maritime (ocean) shipping and trade. The major battles took place in Canada and the Great Lakes region of the United States.

In 1846 the United States went to war with Mexico. The Mexican War (1846–1848) was fought mainly over control of lands in the American Southwest. Within two years, the United States had defeated Mexico and gained much new territory in the Southwest.

THE CIVIL WAR

In 1861 the United States was torn in two. The Southern states—called the Confederate States of America—split from the Northern states, called the Union. The two sides fought one of history's bloodiest wars,

Union soldiers and their commanders pose for a photograph at the beginning of the Civil War. The Union army fought to keep the United States a united country.

Union and Confederate soldiers met in bloody combat during the Civil War's Battle of Bull Run in 1861.

the Civil War (1861–1865). Sometimes brother fought against brother on the battlefield.

When the Civil War began, the U.S. Army (fighting for the North) had only about 16,000 troops. So President Abraham Lincoln called for volunteer soldiers. Within a few weeks, the number of troops rose to 500,000. The South formed its own army during the war.

On the battlefield, soldiers fired at each other using rifles and big guns such as cannons. Sometimes they used bayonets in hand-to-hand combat. Troops in the cavalry fought one another on horseback.

The biggest cavalry battle of the Civil War took place in June 1863, at Brandy Station, Virginia. There, 9,500 mounted soldiers from the South fought 8,000 mounted soldiers from the North.

The war dragged on for four years. The North won more battles than the South, and Southern forces gradually weakened. In 1865 the South surrendered to the North, ending the war and reuniting the nation.

FIGHTING ON HORSEBACK

In the late 1800s, many white settlers moved into western parts of North America. They took over Native American homelands to create their own farms, towns, railroads, and ranches. The Native Americans fought back, trying to defend their lands and homes. In response, the U.S. government sent cavalrymen to fight the Native Americans. In the days before cars and airplanes, a soldier on horseback was the fastest thing on the battlefield—except for bullets and cannonballs.

A wagon train pushes into the North American West in the late 1800s. As U.S. settlers moved west, they took over Native American lands. Conflicts between the two groups quickly grew violent, and the U.S. Army took on the responsibility of protecting the settlers.

Swords raised, U.S. Army cavalry practice mounted warfare in the North American West. U.S. leaders sent the army to protect settlers during the settlement of the West.

The cavalry fought with rifles, pistols, and swords. After riding into battle, they usually got off their horses for hand-to-hand combat. The Native Americans fought back with bows and arrows, clubs, knives, and guns.

In most cases, the cavalry won the battles easily. But the most famous cavalry battle—the Battle of the Little Bighorn, sometimes called Custer's Last Stand—was a rare U.S. defeat. This battle took place in present-day Montana in 1876. About 2,000 Sioux and Cheyenne warriors, led by Chiefs Crazy Horse and Sitting Bull, killed Lieutenant Colonel George Custer and more than 200 of his men. Even with this loss, the army eventually defeated the Native Americans in the West.

Teddy Roosevelt *(far front left)* with his men, the Rough Riders, in 1898. Roosevelt and the Rough Riders captured San Juan Hill in Cuba during a famous battle of the Spanish-American War.

Also in the late 1800s, the army worked on some nonmilitary projects. For instance, to prevent flooding, it helped build a system of levees, or walls, along the Mississippi River. It constructed lighthouses along the shores of the Great Lakes to keep ships from running into rocks and reefs. Soldiers also built thousands of miles of telegraph lines, a system that allowed people to send electronic messages over long distances.

In 1898 Cuba, an island nation in the Caribbean Sea, wanted independence from Spanish rule. The U.S. Army helped Cuba fight the Spanish in a conflict called the Spanish-American War (1898). The most famous army officer in this war was Lieutenant Colonel Theodore Roosevelt (later president of the United States). He led the heroic 1st U.S. Volunteer Cavalry Regiment.

They were nicknamed the Rough Riders because they were the toughest horseback riders Roosevelt could find.

WORLD WAR I

War began in Europe in 1914, when Germany declared war on many of its neighbors, including Russia to the east and France to the west. England came to France's aid. Soon most of Europe was at war. The conflict was called World War I (1914–1918). The United States got involved in 1917, after German submarines began sinking U.S. ships.

To create a large military force, the United States created a draft—a system for calling young men into military service. Drafted men had to serve. If they didn't, they could be sent to jail. During this war, infantrymen (foot soldiers) often fought from trenches, long ditches dug into the ground. Some soldiers operated new equipment that

This U.S. Army recruitment poster from World War I encourages men to join the army.

had never been used in war before. This equipment included tanks, airplanes, and machine guns.

The Americans arrived in Europe in June 1917. U.S. Army units took part in key battles, including the Meuse-Argonne offensive in 1918. This last battle of the war took place on land between the Argonne Forest and the Meuse River in France. Thousands of U.S. Army troops fought in the battle. Germany soon surrendered and the war ended in the fall of 1918.

WORLD WAR II

By the 1930s, Germany was again threatening its neighbors in Europe. Adolf Hitler and his Nazi Party came to power in Germany. In 1939 Hitler ordered his armies to invade neighboring countries. By mid-1940 Germany had conquered most of Europe. In Asia, Japan was also invading and conquering its neighbors. It took over many islands in the Pacific Ocean and fought a savage war in China. The global conflict was called World War II (1939–1945).

At first, the United States stayed out of the war. Then, on December 7, 1941, Japanese bombers launched a surprise attack on a U.S. naval base at Pearl Harbor, Hawaii. Immediately after the attack, the United States entered the war both in Europe and the Pacific.

Millions of soldiers joined the U.S. Army to help fight the war. Others were drafted. Army soldiers fought with tanks, machine guns, hand grenades, and artillery pieces, or large guns. Some soldiers dropped bombs and shot bullets from airplanes.

AFRICAN AMERICANS IN THE ARMY

African Americans have fought with the U.S. Army throughout its history, starting with the American Revolution. Some African Americans fought in the Civil War. Many of these soldiers had been slaves in the American South. During the war, slaves were given their freedom.

In the late 1800s, two all-black units fought against Native Americans in the American West. These troops were nicknamed Buffalo Soldiers. African American soldiers also fought in World War I and World War II. They had to serve in all-black units, however. They were not allowed to live or work with white soldiers. The army usually didn't give black soldiers important combat jobs. But one group of black pilots, the Tuskegee Airmen *(above),* was allowed to fly combat missions during World War II.

In 1948 President Harry Truman ordered that the army and other branches of the military be integrated. This meant that black and white soldiers were fighting side by side. The army, however, was integrated slowly. By the 1960s, white and black soldiers could serve together.

The modern U.S. Army is fully integrated. Black and white soldiers work together on all levels. Many black soldiers, such as Secretary of State Colin Powell, have reached the highest levels of army leadership.

The U.S. Air Force became an official military branch, separate from the army, in 1947. The army, however, still has an aviation branch.

At the time, the air force, officially called the U.S. Army Air Forces, was part of the U.S. Army.

During World War II, the U.S. Army first invaded North Africa and drove the Nazis and their Italian allies out of Africa. Then the army invaded Italy. Next, U.S. and British soldiers crossed the English Channel, traveling from England to invade the shores of German-held France. General Dwight D. Eisenhower (later president of the United States) commanded the invasion, called D-Day. It took place on June 6, 1944.

U.S. Army troops advance inland at Normandy, France, following the D-Day invasion of World War II.

Army soldiers came ashore in thousands of boats, landing on the beaches of Normandy, France. They fought heroically. Thousands of soldiers died. Eventually, the army drove the Germans out of Paris, France, and captured the German capital of Berlin. Germany surrendered in May 1945, ending the war in Europe.

But fighting continued in the Pacific. Led by General Douglas MacArthur, the army fought many island battles against the Japanese. Large battles took place in the Philippines and on the Japanese island of Okinawa. Eventually, the United States defeated the Japanese. World War II ended in September 1945.

KOREA AND VIETNAM

In June 1950, North Korea invaded South Korea. The United States sent army troops to help South Korea.

During the war, the advantage seesawed back and forth. Finally, in 1953, the Korean War (1950–1953) was called a draw, with no real winner. U.S. troops still remain in South Korea to help keep the peace.

In the 1960s and 1970s, the U.S. Army fought in Vietnam in Southeast Asia. This conflict was called the Vietnam War.

Members of an army artillery battalion fire on an enemy position during the Korean War.

U.S. Army helicopter crews patrol the area around a base camp, providing air support for infantrymen during the Vietnam War.

During the war, U.S. troops fought with South Vietnam against troops from North Vietnam. The enemy fighters hid in jungles and used guerrilla tactics, such as ambushes (surprise attacks) and hand-placed bombs. These tactics made the fight hard and deadly for U.S. troops. The army suffered many casualties (soldiers killed or wounded). Eventually, the United States withdrew its troops from Vietnam, and North Vietnam won the war.

MIDDLE EAST CONFLICTS

In the late 1900s, the army turned its attention to other trouble spots around the world. In 1990 the Middle Eastern nation of Iraq, led by Saddam Hussein, invaded its neighbor Kuwait. The United States and its allies came to Kuwait's rescue. In the war that followed, called the Persian Gulf War (1991), the army used "smart weapons" for the very first time. These laser- and computer-guided bombs could strike military targets precisely. After five weeks of bombing and a five-day ground war, the U.S.-led forces drove the Iraqi army out of Kuwait.

Meanwhile, many terrorist groups were operating in the Middle East. On September 11, 2001, a group of terrorists called al-Qaeda hijacked airplanes and crashed them into buildings in New York City and Washington, D.C. About 3,000 Americans were killed in the attacks. Al-Qaeda was headquartered in Afghanistan and protected by the government there. Soon after the September 11 attacks, the U.S. Army attacked Afghanistan's government and the al-Qaeda fighters.

In 2003 army soldiers returned to the Middle East. Saddam Hussein was still in charge of Iraq. The United States wanted him out of power. Army units easily pushed past the Iraqi army and into the capital city of Baghdad.

On December 13, 2003, U.S. Army soldiers captured Hussein, who was hiding in an underground room near his hometown of Tikrit, Iraq. The capture, carried out by members of the 4th Infantry Division, was a major U.S. victory. The army keeps working in Iraq, helping to rebuild the country.

A U.S. soldier from the 4th Infantry Division lifts the lid to the entrance of Saddam Hussein's hideout.

chapter TWO

RECRUITMENT

LOOKING FOR ADVENTURE? Want to
serve your country? Looking for a rewarding experience
between high school and college? Want to be a career
soldier? Those who would like to be part of the world's
most powerful military force can join the U.S. Army.

There are several ways to join the U.S. Army. Some
people join Army Active Duty, which means they enter
the army as full-time soldiers. Others join the Army
Reserve or National Guard, which means they serve
part-time while they go to school or work in another job.

Some people join the army as officers. Officers are the army's leaders. They make decisions about military strategy and command other soldiers in battle. Most soldiers who want to become officers must attend a special officer training school.

New soldiers are called recruits. Army recruits must be between the ages of 17 and 35. They must be U.S. citizens or registered aliens (citizens of other countries living legally in the United States).

The modern U.S. Army is all volunteer. Soldiers are no longer drafted into the army or other branches of military service. (If necessary, the U.S. Congress can create a draft.) About 3 out of every 20 recruits are female.

Two recruits take the U.S. Army oath of enlistment.

They must also be in good health and good shape. When recruits sign up for the army, they must agree to spend at least two years as an active-duty soldier.

Before enlisting, recruits take a test that measures their skills and intelligence. This test is called the Armed Services Vocational Aptitude Battery (ASVAB). It is a three-hour, multiple-choice exam that tests recruits' reading and math skills, as well as their knowledge of mechanics and electronics. There are 200 questions in all. Based on the test results, the army tries to match each recruit with a job the person

A medical officer checks a recruit's eyesight. Recruits must have good eyesight to work as pilots and to work in some other army jobs.

Cadets, or military students, from the U.S. Military Academy
at West Point, New York, practice marching. Graduating cadets
will serve as army officers.

wants and is well suited for. Sometimes, the army
encourages recruits to take certain jobs it needs to fill.

People who want to become U.S. Army officers must
be college graduates. Officer candidates must get good
grades in college. They must also have strong
leadership skills.

Officer candidates have a choice of several training
programs. Many of the nation's top officer candidates
study at the U.S. Military Academy at West Point,
New York. West Point is one of the country's top
schools. College students can join the Army Reserve
Officer Training Corps (ROTC). The ROTC trains
future officers while they are in college. Officer
Candidate School (OCS) is a twelve-week course
for college graduates.

UNIFORMS

ARMY UNIFORMS come in many styles. The two basic categories are dress uniforms and combat uniforms.

DRESS UNIFORM

Soldiers wear dress uniforms at special ceremonies, such as parades and flag raisings. Dress uniforms include a green suit jacket, green dress pants, a light-green shirt, dress shoes, and a beret. Female soldiers sometimes wear skirts with their dress uniforms, sometimes pants. When working in an office, soldiers wear a less formal dress uniform. It has the same green shirt and pants, but it is usually worn without a jacket and tie.

BATTLE DRESS UNIFORM

The army work and combat uniform is called the battle dress uniform, or BDU. It is a camouflage uniform (designed to blend in with a natural background) with pants that tuck into the tops of the soldier's boots. On top, soldiers wear long-sleeve button-down shirts. They also wear a utility belt that holds weapons and other equipment. Depending on the soldier's job, he or she will wear either a helmet or a soft-brimmed hat with this uniform.

COLD-WEATHER BDU

In cold weather, soldiers wear "winter greens," which are BDUs made of heavy material, with a combat jacket for extra warmth.

WARM-WEATHER BDU

In hot summer months, soldiers wear summer BDUs, which are made of lightweight material. Soldiers wear desert BDUs (tan colored) in locations such as Iraq.

THE ARMY SONG:
"THE ARMY GOES ROLLING ALONG"

March along, sing our song
with the army of the free.
Count the brave,
count the true,
who have fought to victory.
We're the army and proud of our name;
We're the army and proudly proclaim:

First to fight for the right,
and to build the nation's might,
And the army goes rolling along.
Proud of all we have done,
Fighting till the battle's won.
And the army goes rolling along....

ARMY BENEFITS

Soldiers in the U.S. Army help defend the United States. In return, the U.S. Army helps soldiers by giving them many benefits. The army helps soldiers develop skills that will help them later in life and in their careers. For instance, a soldier can learn to be a mechanic, a pilot, or a computer technician in the army. The army also gives soldiers free food and housing while they are enlisted.

It pays soldiers' travel and medical expenses. Soldiers also earn a paycheck—around $1,100 a month to start.

Another great benefit is help in paying for college or paying off college loans. Four programs help army soldiers receive a college education. The first is the Montgomery GI Bill and College Fund, which pays soldiers up to $50,000 toward college fees. The College Loan Repayment Program gives soldiers up to $65,000 to pay off previous college loans. The Earned College Credit Program allows soldiers to earn college credits while serving in the army. That is, their army experiences and training count as college classes. Finally, the Concurrent Admissions Program allows soldiers to apply to college while they are in the army.

Two recruits take an exam as part of their basic training. In addition to military training, the army will help soldiers pay for a college education.

If the soldier is accepted, the college will hold a place for that person until after the soldier leaves the army.

ARMY RESERVE AND NATIONAL GUARD

Many people join the army as reservists, or part-time soldiers. Reservists serve one weekend a month and two weeks each year, usually at a base near home. Many men and women who serve in the Army Reserve are full-time students.

Others join the National Guard, which also is a part-time army unit. Each U.S. state has its own National Guard. State governors can call the units into action in times of state or local emergencies.

Reservists and members of the National Guard must agree to become full-time soldiers during a national emergency or other times of need, such as during wartime. During and after the 2003 war in Iraq, many reserve and National Guard units were called into active duty. The requirements for joining the Army Reserve or National Guard are the same as those for joining the U.S. Army as an active-duty soldier.

A reservist chains down a vehicle for transport inside a C-130 aircraft.

THE ARMY GENERAL ORDERS

The Army General Orders are the three rules of being a soldier. The rules are:

1. I will guard everything within the limits of my post and quit my post only when properly relieved.

2. I will obey my special orders and perform all of my duties in a military manner.

3. I will report violations of my special orders, emergencies, and anything not covered in my instructions to the commander of the relief.

A CAREER IN THE ARMY

Not everyone who enlists in the army returns to civilian (nonmilitary) life after a few years. Some men and women decide to become career soldiers. They choose army work as their permanent, long-term jobs. When their enlistment ends, these soldiers reenlist again and again. In this way, many soldiers serve for twenty years or more.

An army career offers many benefits. The army pays career soldiers a salary, which increases over time. The army also pays soldiers' medical bills, travel expenses, and other expenses. After twenty years, career soldiers can retire with a full pension (retirement pay and health-care benefits).

chapter THREE

TRAINING

DIFFERENT RECRUITS go through different types of training in the army, depending on their jobs. But all recruits must go through basic combat training. After enlisting, basic training is the next step in becoming a soldier. This nine-week course gets recruits into top physical condition and teaches them how to take orders and do things quickly. Recruits learn how to be soldiers. The teacher at basic training is the drill sergeant.

Basic training takes place in several locations. These locations include Fort Jackson, South Carolina; Fort Knox, Kentucky; Fort Leonard Wood, Missouri; Fort Benning, Georgia; and Fort Sill, Oklahoma.

Many recruits try to get into top-notch physical condition before reporting for basic training. They run long distances and do plenty of push-ups and sit-ups. To be really prepared, some recruits memorize all the army ranks, from private to general.

After arriving at basic training, recruits are measured for boots and a uniform. They get medical vaccinations (shots that prevent disease). Male recruits get haircuts. Recruits also take more tests, such as eye, health, and fitness tests.

LIFE AT BASIC TRAINING

The day starts early at basic training. When the bugler blows a tune called "Reveille" at 5:00 in the morning (sometimes 4:30), recruits must snap awake and get moving. Lights out is 9:00 P.M. Between those hours, recruits march and

A group of female recruits stands at attention for a morning inspection.

drill. They practice carrying their rifles in different positions. They turn in step with other marching recruits and throw their rifles from shoulder to shoulder with precision, at exactly the same time as everyone else in line. And they learn to look sharp doing it.

Recruits run obstacle courses and learn how to shoot their rifles. During the last few weeks of basic training, they receive field training. In this training, recruits learn how to cope with battlefield conditions. They learn how to dig a trench, pitch a tent and live in it for days at a

(Bottom) Recruits bark out their names after completing an obstacle course during basic training. (Top) During a field training exercise, a female recruit communicates with a helicopter using hand signals.

DRILL SERGEANTS ARE CIVILIZED

Drill sergeants are famous for yelling and screaming. TV shows and movies sometimes show frightening scenes of drill sergeants screaming at, punishing, and insulting recruits. It's true, basic training is rough, and drill sergeants can be tough. A drill sergeant might make a recruit do extra push-ups. A drill sergeant will never strike a recruit.

time, and cross streams and rivers. Depending on where their base is located, they might march through forests, deserts, or swamps. The recruits might scale cliffs and climb mountains—all to get them ready for the hardships of war.

One of the most important things recruits learn is how to get along with others. For many recruits, basic training is their first time away from home. It might be their first experience with people of other races, religions, or backgrounds. Basic training teaches recruits to work with others as a team.

Recruits complete basic training by passing a test (taken both in a classroom and outdoors). The test shows they have learned their lessons and are ready to become full-time soldiers. Recruits have to show that they can take apart, put together, clean, and fire a rifle; that they have learned hand-to-hand combat; and that they know how to read a map and put on a gas mask.

TOOLS OF THE TRADE

HERE'S A QUICK LOOK at the equipment, simple and complex, that makes the U.S. Army such a powerful fighting force.

M16A2 RIFLE

The standard-issue rifle for a foot soldier is the M16A2 *(right)*. At just under eight pounds, it is tough and lightweight. The M16A2 has an adjustable sight, a viewing device that makes it easier for the shooter to hit targets. It holds 30 rounds, or bullets, and can be accurate up to a half mile from a target. The rifle is 40 inches long. Half of that length is the barrel.

M21 SNIPER WEAPON SYSTEM

Snipers—the very best shots in the army—shoot with the M21 Sniper Weapon System. This is a rifle with a telescopic sight attached. The sight magnifies, or enlarges, what the sniper can see. It helps snipers hit targets as far away as three-quarters of a mile.

ARMORED VEHICLES

The army's two main armored vehicles are the M1A2 Abrams battle tank *(left)* and the M3 Bradley Fighting Vehicle.

The Abrams, with a crew of four, is the best tank in the world. It goes faster, has stronger armor, and packs more of a punch with its guns than other tanks. Its main gun is a cannon. The Bradley is a smaller tank, designed to carry soldiers across the battlefield. It operates with a crew of three, with room for eight passengers.

Aircraft
In combat, the air force and navy provide most U.S. air power. But the army does have its own aircraft. It has attack helicopters, such as Apaches *(left)* and Blackhawks. It also has cargo and transport helicopters, such as Chinooks, for moving equipment and troops. The army also has cargo planes and transport planes.

Artillery
The top gun in the artillery is the 155mm howitzer. Its barrel is seven inches across (so are its shells). Big guns can hit targets many miles away.

Smart Weapons
The army uses many unmanned smart weapons, which are aimed and guided to their targets by computers. Computer-guided weapons such as Tomahawk missiles can destroy specific military targets without harming the buildings next door.

After basic training, however, soldiers' training is not complete. Next comes Advanced Individual Training (AIT). During this two-month (or longer) course, soldiers learn to do the specific jobs they'll perform while serving in the army. At AIT, soldiers are trained in many fields, such as communications, construction, vehicle repair, police work, electronics work, nursing, and more.

OFFICER TRAINING

The leaders in the military are called officers. Most officers start their military service by enrolling in a special officer-training program. Enlisted soldiers can also be promoted into officer positions.

Officers promoted from the enlisted ranks are called noncommissioned officers. Officers who attend officer-training schools are called commissioned officers. A third kind of officer, a warrant officer, ranks higher than a noncommissioned officer but lower than a commissioned officer. Warrant officers are usually enlisted soldiers who get promoted because they have specialized skills. For instance,

ARMY PROTOCOL

An old army saying goes: "There are three ways to do something: the right way, the wrong way, and the army way." The army has a proper way to do just about everything. For instance, the brim of a soldier's cap must be worn level with the ground, not pointing up or down. A soldier's bed must be made with the sheets folded a special way at the corners. Soldiers must obey all orders, even if they seem like bad ideas.

During training, recruits and officer candidates alike learn army protocol—how to do everything correctly according to army rules and regulations, or "by the book."

many pilots become warrant officers. The U.S. Army offers four ways to become a commissioned officer.

RESERVE OFFICER TRAINING CORPS (ROTC)

The army offers Reserve Officer Training Corps programs at many U.S. colleges and universities. (Some high schools offer junior ROTC programs that prepare students for college ROTC.) To enroll in ROTC, a student must be between 17 and 21 years old, enrolled in a college with an ROTC program, and a U.S. citizen.

ROTC cadets march in formation at Fort Lewis in Washington. Most U.S. Army officers train through the ROTC program.

> ROTC has produced more than 500,000 lieutenants. Famous ROTC graduates include Secretary of State Colin Powell and NBA basketball coach Lenny Wilkins.

Courses—including leadership development and military skills classes—are taught both in the classroom and out in the field (outdoors). Students can take ROTC courses for up to two years without any obligation to join the army. After that, students must commit to serve. Upon graduation from ROTC, soldiers enter the army as lieutenants. Most army officers (three out of four) are trained through the ROTC program.

West Point cadets (students) practice marksmanship. Besides classroom study, cadets receive hands-on combat training.

U.S. MILITARY ACADEMY (WEST POINT)

Founded in 1802, the U.S. Military Academy in West Point, New York, is a four-year college. It is one of the best colleges in the world, and many of its graduates have gone on to become U.S. leaders. It is very difficult to get into West Point, however.

Cadets celebrate their graduation from West Point.

To apply, candidates need a letter of nomination from a congressional representative. Candidates must be between 17 and 23 years of age, a U.S. citizen, and unmarried. They must also have graduated near the top of their high school class.

West Point and other military-school students are called cadets. In the classroom, cadets study military history and tactics, mathematics, engineering, foreign languages and cultures, and communications. Cadets also go through an intense physical fitness program. "Every cadet an athlete" is an academy motto. West Point graduates must serve in the army for at least five years before returning to civilian life.

OFFICER CANDIDATE SCHOOL

Officer Candidate School is a graduate program. Students must already have a four-year college degree to attend this school. They must also be enlisted in the army, be between 19 and 29 years old, and be U.S. citizens. Students at the school attend officer basic training and then 14 weeks of tough field and classroom training. Officer Candidate School is located at Fort Benning, Georgia. In the classroom, officer candidates learn leadership skills and how to command groups of soldiers. Outdoors, they learn to survive under the harshest conditions, both on land and water. Graduates of Officer Candidate School become army lieutenants.

Officer cadets cautiously approach a clearing during a field training exercise at Officer Candidate School.

DIRECT COMMISSION

People who are already lawyers, doctors, priests, or ministers can join the army as officers. They already have specialized skills the army needs.

Lawyers serve in the Judge Advocate General's Corps (JAG—the army's legal division). They handle legal work such as trying or defending soldiers who are accused of crimes. Doctors work in the Army Medical Corps, taking care of sick and wounded soldiers. Priests and other

An army chaplain spends time with a wounded soldier. Chaplains and other professionals may enter the army as officers.

religious leaders work in the Army Chaplain Corps, where they provide spiritual guidance to soldiers.

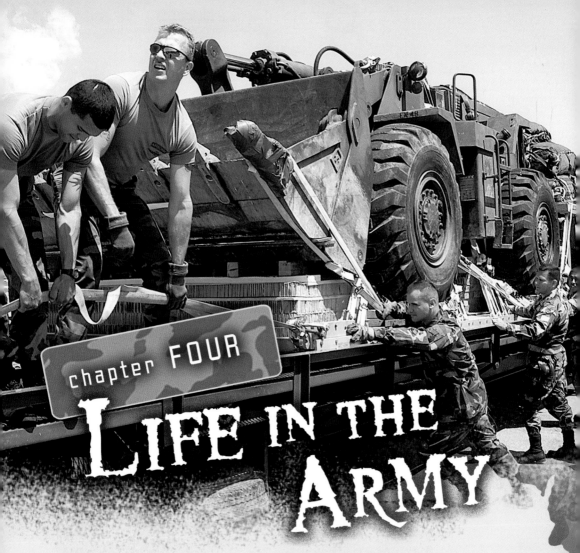

chapter FOUR

LIFE IN THE ARMY

MANY PEOPLE WHO ENLIST in the U.S. Army want to be infantrymen. They want to fight in combat. Foot soldiers must learn to expertly handle their weapons. They must learn to survive outdoors under the most difficult conditions. Infantrymen must become experts in fighting, including hand-to-hand combat. Men can choose to become foot soldiers as their main army job. However, women are not allowed to serve as foot soldiers.

The very best foot soldiers can join the ranks of the army's special combat units, which perform the most dangerous military missions. Tops among these units are the Rangers and the Airborne.

The Ranger motto is "Rangers Lead the Way," and Rangers are often the first soldiers onto the battlefield. Ranger training is very hard. Only a few of those who try to become Rangers make it.

A U.S. Army Ranger candidate demonstrates his endurance and water survival skills during a drill.

The Airborne is another army special combat unit. Members of the Airborne parachute into battlefields and behind enemy lines by jumping out of airplanes. Their training is tough too.

But not everyone who joins the army becomes a foot soldier. The army needs people to perform many different jobs. People interested in police work can learn about law enforcement. Those who want an

Airborne paratroopers practice jumping from a Blackhawk helicopter in Italy.

The lieutenant operating the machine gun on top of this Abrams tank serves in the U.S. Army's armored division.

office job can work in the army's administration or finance department. Those who want to work with big guns can join the artillery. Army engineers and construction workers design and construct buildings, bridges, and roads. Those who want to work with tanks head for the armor division. Others can be missile repairmen or repairwomen. The army also needs mechanics to repair engines. People who like music can try out for an army band. Those with steady hands can handle ammunition. The army also needs recruits who are good with computers. Medical assistants, car and truck drivers, gas station attendants—you name it, the army needs them all.

Many U.S. soldiers live in barracks like these on bases in the United States and around the world.

A DAY IN THE LIFE

Most soldiers live on an army base, which is almost like a small city. The U.S. Army has bases all over the world. Soldiers eat for free in a cafeteria called a mess hall. They sleep, without paying rent, in a barracks, which is a large dormitory building. Some married soldiers live on base in houses or apartments. Others live off base. Men and women live apart on army bases, but these soldiers work together.

All army bases have central parade grounds, where ceremonies are held. All bases also have a headquarters building, where clerks and officers work. Not all bases are the same, though. For instance, some bases are used for helicopter training or tank repair. Some have special equipment such as radar, used to detect objects such as enemy ships and planes. The types of buildings on each base depend on the work that goes on there.

For some soldiers, life on a base can be fairly routine. For those with clerical jobs, for instance, the typical day can resemble that of civilian office workers. These soldiers get up in the morning, eat breakfast, work till noon, eat lunch, work all afternoon, and eat supper. They have the rest of the day and night to themselves.

Not all army jobs are that predictable, however. A member of the military police (MP), for example, may work at any hour, any day of the week. He or she might work all night on the graveyard shift and sleep all day.

These MPs guard an entrance to the Fort Lewis army base in Washington State.

49

INSIGNIA

EVERYONE IN THE ARMY HAS A RANK, or position of authority. Soldiers with higher ranks command those with lower ranks. Soldiers must always follow orders given by those who outrank them.

The lowest rank in the army is private E-1. Recruits start at that rank after enlistment. If privates do what they are told and do their jobs well, they will be promoted to a higher rank. They will receive more pay and more responsibilities. Below are some army ranks and their insignias, or symbols, from lowest to highest.

ENLISTED PERSONNEL

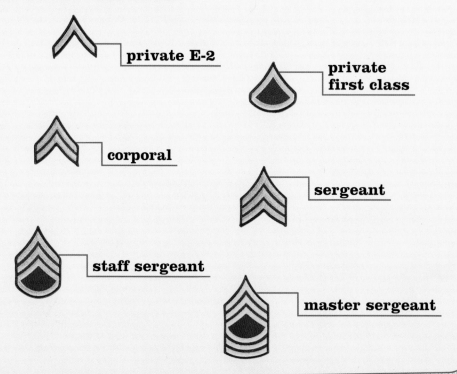

private E-2

private first class

corporal

sergeant

staff sergeant

master sergeant

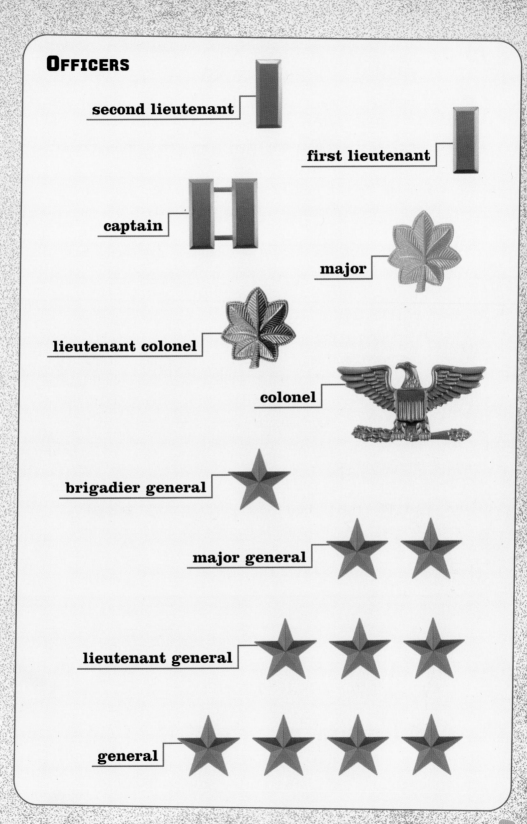

OFFICERS

second lieutenant

first lieutenant

captain

major

lieutenant colonel

colonel

brigadier general

major general

lieutenant general

general

SERVICEWOMEN AND THE 2003 WAR IN IRAQ

Three of the most famous soldiers of the 2003 war in Iraq were women. On March 23, 2003, an Iraqi unit attacked a U.S. convoy (group of trucks). Eleven U.S. soldiers were killed in the attack. The survivors were taken prisoner by the Iraqis.

Nineteen-year-old Private First Class Jessica Lynch, an army clerk from Palestine, West Virginia, was one of the prisoners. She had been wounded in the attack, with broken bones in both legs and one arm. The Iraqis held Lynch in a hospital for three weeks. After an Iraqi citizen told the Americans where Lynch was being held, U.S. soldiers rescued her. After three months in army hospitals, Lynch returned home to West Virginia.

Another soldier in the ambushed convoy was 30-year-old Specialist Shoshana Johnson, who came from El Paso, Texas. She worked in the army as a cook. During the ambush, Johnson was shot in both ankles. The Iraqis took her prisoner and held her with six other U.S. soldiers. U.S. Marines finally rescued Johnson and the other prisoners three weeks after their capture. Johnson was treated for her injuries and returned home to Texas.

Private First Class Lori Piestewa was not as lucky. A Native American mother of two, Piestewa was killed during the March 23 ambush. She was a member of the Hopi people and lived in Tuba City, Arizona. In the history of the U.S. military, she was the first Native American female army soldier to be killed in action.

The schedule can change without warning. For example, if a general is coming to base and needs extra protection, MPs might have to work long hours.

LIFE DURING WARTIME

During times of war, a day in the life of a soldier can become chaotic. There is no telling where the soldier will sleep, or even if he or she will sleep. It is one thing to practice helicopter repair in a hangar (a large garage for aircraft) but quite another to repair a bullet-torn chopper just back from battle.

Wars have different settings, and soldiers don't always know what to expect. The Vietnam War was fought in the jungle. During the 2003 war in Iraq, army soldiers faced many different obstacles. Sandstorms pelted the soldiers as they moved through the Iraqi desert. The blowing sand made it

A U.S. Army private repairs a communication line within Kirkuk Air Base, Iraq, during the 2003 war.

difficult for soldiers to breathe. The sand also clogged up machinery, such as tanks and other vehicles. Equipment broke down, and soldiers had to repair it. Soldiers also had problems telling the difference between friendly and unfriendly Iraqis, who usually dressed the same. Sometimes soldiers had to wait until they were being shot at to know who the enemy was.

Members of an army armored battalion celebrate success in Iraq.

THE FUTURE OF THE ARMY

What will the U.S. Army be like in ten years? In one hundred years? Seeing clearly into the future is difficult. Still, there are some things we can be sure of.

The army, like most other military branches, will probably use more computer-guided weapons, including missiles, artillery, and tanks. Weapons systems will grow even deadlier to the enemy—but safer for any civilians who might be nearby. With new technology, the future army will be able to get soldiers on and off the battlefield more quickly. The army's armored vehicles—tanks and personnel carriers—will be stronger and faster than ever. The same will be true of army aircraft, from attack helicopters to cargo planes.

The U.S. Army will be ready for combat in the jungle, the desert, the city, or the countryside. Young Americans will continue to enlist in the army and continue to improve their skills. More and more women will join the army alongside the men. In short, army troops will continue to serve their country proudly and will always be ready to fight.

STRUCTURE

THE BASIC ARMY UNIT IS THE SQUAD, made up of 10 soldiers. Three or four squads make up a platoon, two or more platoons make up a company, and two or more companies make up a battalion. Groups of battalions make up a brigade. Groups of brigades make up a division. Two or more divisions make up a corps. Two or more corps make up a theater of operations.

Each of these units is led by an officer: a staff sergeant for a squad, a lieutenant for a platoon, a captain for a company, a lieutenant colonel for a battalion, a colonel for a brigade, a major general for a division, a lieutenant general for a corps, and a general for a theater of operations. Generals report to the army chief of staff and to the secretary of the army. These officials report to the secretary of defense, who reports to the president.

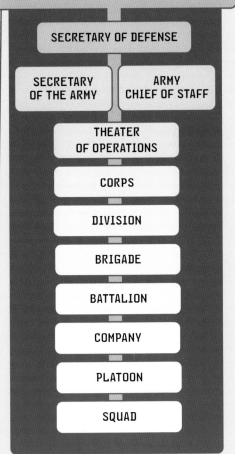

PRESIDENT OF THE UNITED STATES

SECRETARY OF DEFENSE

SECRETARY OF THE ARMY

ARMY CHIEF OF STAFF

THEATER OF OPERATIONS

CORPS

DIVISION

BRIGADE

BATTALION

COMPANY

PLATOON

SQUAD

TIMELINE

1775   The Continental Army is founded.

1783   The U.S. Army defeats the British in the American Revolution.

1812–1815   The U.S. Army fights the British in the War of 1812.

1846–1848   The United States defeats Mexico in the Mexican War, acquiring a large part of the American Southwest after the war's end.

1861–1865   The U.S. Army fights on the side of the Union (North) and helps it win the Civil War.

1876   Lieutenant Colonel George Custer and his cavalry are defeated at the Battle of the Little Bighorn.

1898   The U.S. Army drives the Spanish out of Cuba in the Spanish-American War.

1917–1918   The U.S. Army fights in World War I, helping defeat Germany.

1941   The United States enters World War II.

1944   The U.S. Army participates in the D-Day invasion of German-occupied Normandy, France, then drives the Germans out of Paris, the French capital city.

1945   Germany surrenders in May, ending World War II in Europe. Japan surrenders in August, ending World War II.

1950–1953   The U.S. Army assists South Korea in its war with North Korea.

1964–1973   The U.S. Army assists South Vietnam in its war with North Vietnam.

1991   In the Persian Gulf War, the U.S. Army helps drive Iraqi troops out of Kuwait.

2001   The U.S. Army begins its fight against al-Qaeda terrorists.

2003   The U.S. Army fights in Iraq to remove Saddam Hussein from power.

GLOSSARY

ammunition: material such as bullets and shells fired from guns and artillery pieces

artillery: large firearms such as howitzers

camouflage: patterned clothing or other material that allows soldiers to blend in with a natural background

casualties: soldiers lost during warfare due to death, injury, sickness, or capture

civilian: a person not involved in military service

combat: active fighting in warfare

draft: a system in which the government requires civilians to join the military

guerrillas: small groups of soldiers who make sudden sneak attacks, often behind enemy lines. Guerrillas use unconventional weapons and tactics.

infantry: soldiers trained and equipped to fight on foot

insignia: a badge or symbol to show military rank

integrate: to allow people of different backgrounds to live or work together, such as black and white soldiers serving together in the army

recruit: a newly enlisted soldier

terrorism: the use of violence, such as bombing, to terrify civilians

FAMOUS PEOPLE

Clara Barton (1821–1912) Barton was born in Massachusetts. She worked during the Civil War as an army nurse. She greatly improved systems for bringing medicine and bandages to wounded soldiers. She also started programs to help find soldiers who were missing in action. After the war, Barton founded the American Red Cross.

Dwight D. Eisenhower (1890–1969) Known as Ike, army general Eisenhower was born in Texas. After commanding the invasion of Europe during World War II, Eisenhower was twice elected president, in 1952 and 1956. "I Like Ike" was his campaign slogan, and he easily won both elections.

Theodor "Dr. Seuss" Geisel (1904–1991) The creator of classic children's books such as *How the Grinch Stole Christmas, The Cat in the Hat,* and *Hop on Pop,* Geisel was born in Massachusetts. He enlisted in the army during World War II. He worked as a writer and cartoonist for the army's information and education division. He also wrote promotional films for the army's Signal Corps.

Ulysses S. Grant (1822–1885) General (and future president) Ulysses S. Grant led the Union army throughout the Civil War. He was born in Ohio, the son of an Ohio leather maker. He attended the U.S. Military Academy at West Point, New York, graduated in the middle of his class, and fought in the Mexican War. When the Civil War began, Grant was working for his father in Illinois. The governor of Illinois appointed Ulysses Grant to command a group of volunteer soldiers. He did such a good job that he quickly rose through the army ranks. He served as U.S. president from 1869 to 1877.

Robert E. Lee (1807–1870) Commander of the Confederate forces during the Civil War, Lee was born in Virginia. He graduated from the U.S. Military Academy. He also fought in the Mexican War. He opposed the South breaking away from the United States, and he opposed slavery, which many Southerners supported. But he fought for the South because he was loyal to his home state of Virginia. He led his army to several victories in Virginia before being defeated at Gettysburg, Pennsylvania. He surrendered to Ulysses Grant in 1865, bringing the Civil War to an end.

Willie Mays (born 1931) Born in Alabama, Mays played baseball for the New York and San Francisco Giants and the New York Mets. A hall-of-famer, Mays led the National League in home runs four times. He was twice the league's Most Valuable Player. After his rookie season in 1951, he served in the army for two years but did not see combat. He returned to baseball for the 1954 season.

Colin Powell (born 1937) Born in New York City, Powell entered the army as a lieutenant after attending an ROTC program at the City College of New York. He saw combat in the Vietnam War. He rose through the ranks and, in April 1989, was promoted to four-star general. In August 1989, he became the youngest-ever chairman of the Joint Chiefs of Staff (the head military adviser to the president) and the first African American ever to hold that position. Since 2001 Powell has been the U.S. secretary of state.

Elvis Presley (1935–1977) Called the King of Rock and Roll, Presley was born in Mississippi. He was the world's number-one recording star when he was drafted into the army in 1958. Upon joining the army, Presley's monthly salary fell from the $100,000 he was making as an entertainer to the $78 he made as a soldier. Stationed in Germany, he served until 1960. Presley went on to become a film star in the 1960s and continued to make hit records until his death.

Sarah Emma Edmonds Seelye (1841–1898) A master of disguise, Seelye was born in New Brunswick, Canada. She enlisted in the U.S. Army as a man named Franklin Thompson. Pretending to be a male nurse, she served during several Civil War battles. When, after a year of duty, the army learned she was a woman, it put her to work spying on the enemy. She spied on the Confederacy, sometimes disguised as an African American man, sometimes as a Southern woman.

George Washington (1732–1799) Born in Virginia, Washington fought in the French and Indian War (1754–1763). Afterward, he managed a farm at Mount Vernon, Virginia, and served in the government of Virginia. In 1775, with the Revolutionary War near, American leaders elected Washington commander in chief of the Continental Army. After the United States became independent, Washington became the nation's first president, serving from 1789 to 1797.

BIBLIOGRAPHY

Coffman, Edward M. *The War to End All Wars: The American Military Experience in World War I.* New York: Oxford University Press, 1968.

Cosmas, Graham A. *An Army for Empire: The United States Army in the Spanish-American War.* Shippensburg, PA: White Mane, 1994.

Higginbotham, Don. *The War of American Independence: Military Attitudes, Policies, and Practice, 1763–1789.* New York: Macmillan, 1971.

Holm, Jeanne. *Women in the Military: An Unfinished Revolution.* Novato, CA: Presidio Press, 1992.

McPherson, James M. *Battle Cry of Freedom: The Civil War Era.* New York: Oxford University Press, 1988.

Palmer, Dave R. *Summons of the Trumpet: U.S.-Vietnam in Perspective.* San Rafael, CA: Presidio Press, 1978.

Perret, Geoffrey. *There's a War to Be Won: The United States Army in World War II.* New York: Random House, 1991.

Prucha, Francis Paul. *The Sword of the Republic: The United States Army on the Frontier, 1783–1846.* New York: Macmillan, 1969.

Weigley, Russell F. *History of the United States Army.* Bloomington: Indiana University Press, 1984.

FURTHER READING

Arnold, James. *The Civil War.* Minneapolis: Lerner Publications Company, 2005.

Behrman, Carol. *The Indian Wars.* Minneapolis: Lerner Publications Company, 2005.

Bohannon, Lisa Fredericksen. *The American Revolution.* Minneapolis: Lerner Publications Company, 2004.

Doeden, Matt. *The U.S. Army.* Mankato, MN: Blazers, 2005.

Goldstein, Margaret J. *World War II—Europe.* Minneapolis: Lerner Publications Company, 2004.

Marrin, Albert. *George Washington and the Founding of a Nation.* New York: Dutton Children's Books, 2001.

Roberts, Jeremy. *U.S. Army Special Operations Forces.* Minneapolis: Lerner Publications Company, 2005.

Williams, Barbara. *World War II—Pacific.* Minneapolis: Lerner Publications Company, 2005.

Zwier, Lawrence J., and Matthew S. Weltig. *The Persian Gulf and Iraqi Wars.* Minneapolis: Lerner Publications Company, 2005.

WEBSITES

Goarmy.com
<http://www.goarmy.com>
This site offers extensive information for young people interested in joining the army. The site includes information on basic training, army jobs, ROTC, and more.

Military.com
<http://www.military.com>
This site offers extensive information about the army, as well as the other branches of the military. Visitors can learn about getting an education through the military, careers in the military, recruiting, and news. They can also subscribe to the Military.com newsletters.

The United States Army Home Page
<http://www.army.mil>
This site includes news and information regarding recruitment, the Army Reserve, ROTC programs, army history, veterans' affairs, and more.

United States Military Academy at West Point
<http://www.usma.edu>
This site includes information about classes and activities at West Point, admissions procedures, and biographies of famous graduates. Information is also available for those who want to visit the school.

INDEX

ABOUT THE AUTHOR

Michael Benson is the former editor of the *Military Technical Journal*. He is also the author of thirty books, including *The Encyclopedia of the JFK Assassination* and *Complete Idiot's Guide to NASA*. Originally from Rochester, New York, he is a graduate of Hofstra University. He lives with his wife and two children in Brooklyn, New York.

PHOTO ACKNOWLEDGMENTS

The images in this book are used with the permission of:
© National Archives, pp. 8, 9, 10, 12, 13, 18, 19; courtesy of the U.S. Army pp. 4, 5, 21, 34 (bottom), 45, 53, 54; © Defense Visual Information Center pp. 6, 22, 23, 24, 25, 26 (both), 27 (both), 29, 30, 33, 34 (top), 35, 36 (both), 37, 39, 40, 41, 42, 43, 44, 46, 47, 48, 49; Library of Congress, pp. 7 [LC-USZ62-3291], 11 [LC-USZC4-1796], 14 [LC-USZ62-75155], 15 [LC-USZC4-10143], 17 [LC-F9-02-4503-330-5]; © U.S. Army Military History Institute, p. 20; © Leif Skoogfors/CORBIS, p. 32; © Todd Strand/ Independent Picture Service, pp. 50 (all), 51 (all).

Cover: © Peter Turnley/CORBIS.

Benson, Michael.

The U.S. Army.

BAKER & TAYLOR